Study Guide
Stepping Out
A Journey of the Soul

Kim Laliberte

Study Guide: Stepping Out – A Journey of the Soul

King's Agenda Publishing

Book Cover Design: Sharon Holt
Internal Layout: John Laliberte
Cover Photo: Istock Photos, Sara Winter

ISBN: 978-0-9977662-1-9 Printed in the United States of America

Other books by Kim Laliberte:

The Call to Follow Jesus, Studies in the Gospel of Mark, WestBow Press, a Division of Thomas Nelson, 2013. Also available at Amazon.com and Barnes & Nobel.

The Acts Project, Volume I (Acts 1-7), available directly from the author through the website www.KingsAgenda.com for purchase.

TABLE OF CONTENTS

Study Guide: Stepping Out – A Journey of the Soul

WELCOME TO THE JOURNEY

I am so excited that this book is in your hands. It says that you really do desire a deeper walk with Jesus and that you want more abundance, joy and healing in your life. I hope it means that you are ready to do the serious work of moving forward. Healing and freedom are on the way!

If you haven't done so already, you will need to purchase the actual book, *Stepping Out, A Journey of the Soul*. Hopefully you already have it. If you've already read it, you'll have a basic understanding of what stepping out and stepping back in looks like. Essentially, *stepping out* is when we move away from Jesus' command to follow in His footsteps and go our own way. *Stepping in* is how God leads us back to Him and the strategies and weapons of war He gives us to both step in and stay in.

You will also need your Bible. Without reading the actual Scriptures spoken of in this book, you might, (no, you will!) miss important insights. If you've already read the book, you know that I fully believe the Bible is where the answers are. That is the life-changing Book. This book and study guide are only that – guides to help you drink your full complement of Living Water.

On the other hand, this study guide is the place where you will learn to know *and* experience His Truth as revealed through the stories, the Scripture verses and the lessons contained in the book. This is where you make them your own. When you have completed this study guide, you will have chronicled your progress in the journey. (If you date each lesson when you complete it, as I suggest, you will see a timeline of your progress.) Your worksheets may become a place where memories are built. As you will learn in the book, *Remembering* is a weapon of war

Study Guide: Stepping Out – A Journey of the Soul

God gives us to teach us to stand firm. This study guide will also become your own personal commentary and depository of information concerning weapons, strategies for living and overcoming --Jesus' way.

So, are you ready? Let's move.

Introduction

Introduction

Whether you do this study on your own or with a group, I hope you will consider me as one of your partners in the journey. Though I am no expert, I have walked and am continuing to walk this journey in my own life. I will never give up on seeking more depth with Jesus and I hope you won't either.

Some of these questions will cause you to ponder and pray. I hope you will stop and do it when the Spirit nudges you. Do not race through the principles. It has taken me the better part of a lifetime to learn these questions to ask myself.

If you are doing the study as a group, each of you should be aware that some of the questions might not be immediately shareable with one another. Though you should each work toward openness and vulnerability, some questions and parts of the book may open raw areas in life that are too fresh or too surprising to immediately share. Receive and extend grace here.

Be very careful with the information you are entrusted with in the group. Never, never share anything you hear from a member in the group, outside the group. It is so injurious to people to hear their own pain being talked about or even "prayed over" by people outside the group. By indiscriminate sharing, you could be the person who causes a deep heart wound instead of being part of the healing process. In my leadership capacity, I have known people who were so wounded by this very thing that they left the church. We are carrying each others' hearts here. *Be extremely alert in this area!*

Study Guide: Stepping Out – A Journey of the Soul

As trust grows, you will hopefully be better able to share your experiences. Some areas need to be held as being between you and God until you feel able to share. Do not feel ashamed if others appear more open than you. Each of you may need to consider starring those questions you do not feel able to share the first time through. At the end of the study, take a session and let the starred questions become the discussion.

This study guide is atypical -- unlike other study guides --because I am writing it in the first person, from me to you, as though we were sitting together and talking these things through. I purposefully chose to write this guide this way because the journey of the soul is something personal that we each experience in different ways. But our stories intersect with one another through the binding truth of the Scriptures. We may not know one another, but we are in this journey together. He is with us and is the One who speaks and uses our journey to comfort and encourage others in their journey. May it be so in this case.

> *"Praise be to the God and Father of our Lord Jesus Christ, the Father of compassion and the God of all comfort, who comforts us in all our troubles, so that we can comfort those in any trouble with the comfort we ourselves have received from God."* -- 2 Corinthians 1:3-5

My prayer for you is that the time spent in this book and, most importantly, in His Word, will carry you deeper into His Presence. It is what He longs for and, in the deepest places of your own soul, it is what you also long for. Soul healing is on the way, precious brothers and sisters in Christ.

Kim Laliberte

2018

Chapter 1. You were Meant for More

On page 3 of the book I share with you about other people who also desired a deeper walk with Jesus. During this time in my own life, I prayed something like this: *"Father, more of Jesus. Just give me a deeper walk with Him and I will be satisfied."* Think about one prayer request that you could share with the group related to your own walk with Jesus. Whether with a group or on your own, write it down here and pray over it every time you open this book. Let it be your ongoing request throughout this study.

1. Read the parable of the Good Shepherd in your Bible at John 10:1-18. Review Kim's thoughts on pages 3-4. What insights did you gain as you read the story? Write them here.

2. What insights did you gain from the book's word study of John 10:10 (Pages 4-5)?

3. Based on what insights you learned from Chapter 1, would you say you are living the abundant life Jesus calls you to?

4. Did you have any expectations or misconceptions on what your future would be like by becoming a believer? Describe them here.

Chapter 2. Experiencing the More You were Made For

1. Of the three lifestyles of the believer spoken of on pages 9-11, do any of the three describe your life either in the past or right now? If so, which one(s). Describe in your own words what that looks like.

2. Read Jesus' *job description* found in Isaiah 61:1-4. Which of the jobs mentioned do you need to see Jesus activate in your soul right now? (Page 12-13) If you did the exercise in the book, what insights did you write down?

3. What misconceptions, if any, do see in your walk with God? (You may not see any at this time.)

4. Where are you at in the discussion about the need to get into the battle with God versus expecting God to fight your

battles for you while you wait on the sidelines? This is a critically important question. Answering this honestly from your heart may reveal part of the reason you may not be experiencing the abundant life Jesus spoke of. (Pages 13-14)

5. Consider the continent of your soul prayerfully. (Pages 16-17) What does it look like? Do you see more light or more darkness? If you can, describe what you see. Do not feel defeated if you can't see. All of us suffer from spiritual darkness in some areas of the soul, and getting more light is the process of a Holy God given access to your soul through your surrender over your lifetime. If you are willing and surrendered, He will reveal this truth to you in His time.

6. Of the different meanings for the word *salvation* listed on pages 18-19 (to rescue, restore, deliver, preserve, keep safe, keep from destruction, make whole), which words seem to resonate with your soul? What are the words saying to you concerning either the lack in your life or the fulfillment?

Chapter 3. The Binding Chains

1. As you read about Ebenezer Scrooge and his former business partner, do you see any chains in your own life being forged, "link by link, yard by yard"? Consider habits, idols, habitual sins, addictions and other areas that plague you that you can't seem to let go of? List them here.

2. As you examine your own life, what "respectable sins" do you harbor in your soul? (Pages 23-25)

3. Where are you on the sin continuum mentioned on page 23? Try to be honest with yourself. Is it easier to judge others whose sins are different (and maybe more outward) than yours? Do you see others' sins differently than you see your own?

4. For some time, I did not see my secret sin. It was hidden in the depths of my soul, even as it affected my words, attitudes and actions. It was not until God revealed that these were my sins that I was able to see. Before, I was unable to really call out doubt, unbelief, envy and pride as my sin even though in my head I knew they were sins that we were capable of. I did not recognize the subtle ways these sins were masked. What about you? Are you likewise struggling in this area? Write your thoughts here.

5. What things are robbing you from deeper fellowship with God? List them here.

Chapter 4. Unlocking the Binding Chains

Every time we read to see rather than read to know, the message becomes personal. God will not pile stuff on us, but He will reveal from Scripture principles to incorporate into our walk. He will also reveal sins in our lives in order to help us see, repent and receive forgiveness. This is the way of healing.

1. Review the passages listed on page 29 (Matthew 15, Romans 1 and Mark 6). Make a list of recognizable sins Jesus and Paul speak of. While there is no one place in Scripture where our sin is categorized or listed compactly, these words give us a beginning. Pick 2-3 words from the list you came up with that you might be harboring in your life. Write them here.

2. Page 31 contains a summary of sin in the believer. Review the points and star the areas that need more clarification for you. Jot down your thoughts and questions to discuss with the group.

3. How does the Holy Spirit reveal things in your life? What differences do you note between how He exposes areas of your life needing attention and how you treat yourself when you have failed. (Pages 32-33) Who is more compassionate?

4. How would you define sin? Write out your own definition here along with any Scripture verses you know about the topic. What do they tell you about sin.

5. Do you think you are more of a person who:

(a) Does not always see my sin and thus am in need of God's revealing in my life;

(b) Sees myself as the worst possible sinner who could not possibly be forgiven again; or

(c) Sees myself as living a surrendered life, able to name and repent daily of my specific sins and am able to receive forgiveness and cleansing instantly without going over and over the sins again?

(d) Somewhere in between? (Explain)

I know this is an area most of us need soul work in. Life is challenging enough without having to dredge up daily sins, more negativity and the feeling of constantly feeling under the power. But that is not how God reveals our sin. Since we all sin, we all need His revealing and convicting to lead us to repentance. Part of learning to stand firm and stay the course means we all need the confession of sin to feel the refreshment of forgiveness and new beginnings. It is like breathing the rarefied air of heaven when we take Him at His word and ask forgiveness. Relationship is restored.

Chapter 5. A Painful Betrayal: A Biblical Example

1. In order to become comfortable spotting the difference, write some examples of sins of:

   (a) **Words** – Example: gossip, angry words, words that tear down others.

   (b) **Attitudes** – Example: rebellion, unforgiveness, unbelief.

   (c) **Actions** – Example: Giving in to addictions, abuse, sexual sin, violence.

2. If you did the exercise in the book at page 36, what consequences did you come up with? If you did not do the exercise, read 2 Samuel 12 and note the consequences that you see from David's life after Bathsheba.

3. In 2 Samuel 24:10-14 David takes a census of his men and calls it sin. (Page 37) How does David see sin that might be different than how we see it?

4. There is no single apparent method that God uses to handle our sin. He is God and He knows best even if we cannot see. Sometimes God gives grace instead of a consequence and sometimes He allows the consequences of our actions or the actions of others to fall on us and those around us. Can you think of a time in your life when you clearly experienced one or the other? Share it with the group.

5. Of the three choices the prophet Gad gave David, which would you choose? (Pages 37-38) Why?

Chapter 6. An Orphan's Story

1. Consider Tracy's parable on page 40. I love the picture the story presents. What parallels to that story do you see in your own walk of following Jesus? Do you trust the Guide? Or is it safer to stay in the car instead of moving out?

2. Look at the questions asked by Allen at the writer's conference I attended. How do you respond to them? (Page 41) Hopefully you will have a Kleenex close at hand if you need it!

3. As you read about and consider how I became aware of the "orphan spirit" in my life and how it manifested, do you see any parallels in your life? What are you seeing, hearing or feeling? Write it down here.

The question of how demons intersect with Christians is not a topic most Christians (including me) want to look into. But it is quite possible the level of our freedom in Christ depends on how we see this issue. For me, I wanted to avoid run-ins with the enemy, but my desire for a deeper walk with Jesus was stronger. It was not until I understood this issue that I was able to move into more freedom in my life. Take some time to pray and ponder this issue, being careful to not become so focused on this that you lose focus on Jesus. This will be a prime time where the enemy will whisper in your ear to give up. You might hear things like, "*She doesn't know what she's talking about; forget about this book; It can't help you; you don't need this. Your church doesn't believe this; You're already mature in your walk with God.*" These thoughts would be similar to the ones I had while writing this book. Many of the people I love and serve do not believe this, nor did I until just a few years ago. If this is what you're hearing, please don't give up now. Keep moving forward seeking only Jesus, keeping your focus on Him alone. Remember, as you discuss this issue, not everyone will agree. Again, dispense grace and pray for peace.

4. After reviewing the Scripture verses on page 44, write down your insights from what you read.

Chapter 7. Generational Bondage and Blessing

1. This would be a good time to ponder this question: Why are you seeking a deeper relationship with God? Is it because of what He can do for you or is it for Himself alone? This deserves a thoughtful and honest appraisal. God already knows and will not be angry at your honest response to the question.

2. What is the "warning" and the "promise" you see in Exodus 20:2-6? (Page 47)

3. What do you think Rabbi Schneider's quote on page 49 means? Is there something in your life that needs to be relinquished or given up to grow closer to Jesus? Write about it here.

Study Guide: Stepping Out – A Journey of the Soul

Perhaps you are finding this chapter particularly challenging. Maybe you have lived a godly life, done your best by your children or grandchildren and still do not see the fruit of your walk with Jesus stamped into their lives. You may be experiencing a variety of emotions over this: *anger, resentment, envy, despair, jealousy, depression or shame.* If this does in fact describe you (or even someone you know), try to pinpoint and write down what emotions, thoughts or feelings you are experiencing or have experienced. God reveals to heal and He may be drawing you to express and expose that which you, as a good Christian, feel ashamed to expose. It is as things are brought into the light that they can receive healing. Let the words you write here be between you and God as you confess them and ask for cleansing and help.

4. In the Section entitled *Family Dispositions* on page 51, we speak of a different type of generational bondage. Consider these areas also in your life and write down possibilities that come to you as you work through this part of the journey.

Read aloud the summary of Exodus 20:4-6 on page 52 before leaving this chapter.

Chapter 8. Life of a Biblical Orphan

1. After reading 1 Kings 18-19, what is your assessment of Elijah's orphan status? Was his belief that he was "all alone", the "only one left" a true statement?

2. Review the section **The Power of a Word Curse** on page 54. What does a word curse do in someone's life according to the reading.

3. Consider my point about Mount Horeb being called, "the place of desolation". (Page 55) No doubt you have been there a few times on your journey. Maybe you are there now. Consider the questions on page 55 of the book: *"What are you doing here? Why did you come here? How did you get here? What do you want God to do for you."* How would you answer these questions in your own life?

4. How did God come to Elijah and how did God answer his questions? (Page 56)

5. Summarize my journey from orphan-hood to freedom beginning on page 56, noting how long it took to work and pray through this area. No two journeys are alike and your journey, if this is part of your baggage, may take time. Do not expect immediate freedom, though it may happen that way for you.

6. If an orphan spirit is not part of your journey, consider the steps I took for perhaps a different journey in your soul. Is there anything you can learn from my journey that resonates with some part of yours? Write about it here.

Chapter 9. Stepping Out - My Story

1. Have you ever considered the difference between hearing and listening as it was explained on page 62? Is there a time in your life when you heard clearly from God, but failed to listen? Recap it here. What happened?

2. In remembering a task or assignment you believe God gave you, did you experience difficulty in completing the task? Explain here what happened. What kinds of obstacles did you face? What words were you hearing during this time either in your soul or from others regarding this assignment?

3. On pages 66-67, we talk about how your own words can take you out. How have you experienced this? Describe.

Perhaps you have never considered doubt a sin. I know I didn't fully believe it was. If there is doubt in your soul, and I think most of us have this buried somewhere in us, this is where the enemy will take advantage and might gain a foothold. Keep in mind that if you have been a believer a short time doubts are more normal as your faith is growing and being stretched. But for me, I had been a fervent believer for many years and had not strongly doubted His work in me before this time in my life. Note the connection between the assignment, *"write a book"* and the doubt, *"He will not help me. Maybe He can't be trusted."* Have you experienced this kind of doubt?

4. Look at the definition on page 67. Have you experienced this in your own life on assignments from God. Write the definition. How can understanding this definition can help you in the journey?

I consider this question of deep importance because this could be an area that needs exposure by God's Spirit working in your soul:

5. Are you one who, for whatever reason, does not believe the promises are for you? If so, it's time to take another look at that doctrinal position in your life. Here are some steps to take:

- Begin to pray about this issue
- Go to the Word itself and look for what it says about His faithfulness to keep His promises
- Ask Him to expose anything hidden in you that might keep you from believing His promises
- Think about things like, *"Have I been abandoned; betrayed in some way; do I believe I am alone in the journey; has God forsaken me in some way?"*
- Ask Him to speak to you on these issues

Chapter 10. Unmasking the Enemy

1. Look at the quote by Vicki Burke on page 69. What mirror are you gazing into?

2. What is the birthright Jesus was given at His baptism? (page 71) What is the birthright you are given upon asking Christ into your life? Write them both here.

3. Do you understand the enemy will try to steal your birthright in the same way he tried to steal Jesus'? As you think about this, what attempts have already been made in your life? What did the attempts look like?

4. How did Jesus teach us how to protect our birthright? (Pages 71-72)

5. Write down every definition or commentary listed on page 69 concerning the word "to steal". How does the enemy try to steal from your life? (Pages 73-74)

6. Write down every definition or commentary listed on pages 73-74 concerning the word, "to kill". Have you experienced this in your life? Describe.

7. Write down every definition or commentary listed on page 74 concerning the word, "to destroy". Have you experienced this in any way in your life? Describe.

Chapter 11. The Hidden Serpent Revealed

1. Summarize how the *stare of the cobra* manifests in your life. Can you add any insights about cobras from your own knowledge? Can you recall a time in your life when the stare of the cobra tried to take you out? Describe it here.(Pages 77-78)

2. Summarize how the *asp* manifests in your life. Can you add any insights about asps from your own knowledge? Can you recall a time in your life when the asp tried to take you out? Describe it here.(Page 79)

3. Summarize how the *viper* manifests in your life. Can you add any insights about vipers from your own knowledge? Can you recall a time in your life when the viper tried to take you out? Describe it here.(Pages 79-80)

4. Summarize how the *python* manifests in your life. Can you add any insights about pythons from your own knowledge? Can you recall a time in your life when the python tried to take you out? Describe it here.(Pages 80-81)

5. Just recognizing the type of strike you have encountered may help you prepare to neutralize the attacks. Using the tools Jesus taught us about protecting our birthright (Pages 71-72), how can those tools help you here?

6. Of the areas mentioned, where are you most vulnerable to attack?

Chapter 12. Warnings and Clues

1. Review Isaiah 40:26-31. Jot down your thoughts and comments as you read. What is God's Word saying to you right now through this passage?

2. Is there a warning or clue God may be giving you concerning some area of your life right now? Write about it here.

3. One of the enemy's favorite ploys to take us out is to use other people's words to do the work. Whether well-intentioned or spiteful, the words can broadside you. Has someone come to mind who has been used to pull you out of a task God had given you to do? If so, stop here and follow the words of forgiveness and blessing over the person. I know. It's counter intuitive, isn't it? But by surrendering the pain and cutting the tie, you will be the one to receive the blessing. (Page 87-91)

4. Read Matthew 16:21-23. Jesus looked beyond Peter's words to the source of the words. How can understanding this passage help you incorporate this strategy into your own arsenal? (Page 88)

5. Now it's your turn. Have you or your words unwittingly been the instrument to affect someone else's calling? To my own shame, I have had to consider this area many times and ask God to forgive and heal.

Read aloud the words on pages 90-91, beginning with: "There is some truth…"

Chapter 13. The Man Who Stepped Out

1. As you read through the book of Jonah, what insights do you have?

2. What sins do you see in Jonah from your reading? Catalog them as words, attitudes or actions.

3. Almost from beginning to end, Jonah's soul was in rebellion to God; yet God chose him to bring the message to Nineveh. Likewise, in your life, there may be a task He has assigned to you that no one else can do -- just as Lady Galadriel told Frodo in *Lord of the Rings*, *"This task has been assigned to you, Frodo of the Shire. If you do not complete it, no one will."* Is there some task left unfinished in your life that needs to be reconsidered? Write about it here.

4. Review Jonah's time in the belly of the fish. Perhaps you have had consequence in your life as well that caused you a lot of pain. What insights do you have about this specific time in Jonah's life? What about your own life?

5. Had Jonah not completed his assignment, what do you think might have happened? (Consider Jonah 4:9-11)

Chapter 14. When Warnings and Clues are Not Enough

1. As you read my journal entry (Pages 101-102), what attitude problems and sins do you see in the writings?

2. How would you explain what "hidden sin" is? Do you think people harbor things in their lives they are not aware of? Why doesn't God reveal all these things to us?

3. Of the word studies noted in this chapter, which do you most closely relate to? How do they show up in your life? Of those words you most closely align with, you may need to stop here and confess to God these attitude sins, seeking and receiving His forgiveness and cleansing.

4. Can you think of other ways the enemy can gain a foothold in the soul, other than through attitude sins?

Chapter 15. Failed Warnings

1. Read John 5:1-15. Why do you think Jesus asked the man *if* he wanted to get well?

2. What does Jesus' question (Question 1 above) say about Jesus' own character?

3. What *pools* have replaced Jesus in your life? What are you depending on apart from God to get you to your next step or get you out of a situation you are currently in?

4. What provisions for failure are you holding in your life? Ponder carefully and pray, as you may not see.

5. How are parts of your story similar to the man's story?

6. Review John 5:9-13 to see how sneak attacks can take you out. Have you experienced anything like this in your life? Describe it here.

7. When Jesus saw the man the following day, what words did He have for him? (Page 112) What does this part of the story tell us for our lives today?

Chapter 16. Making and Breaking Contracts with the Enemy

The three questions in this chapter are designed to help us see -- starting with the general idea of how we as God's people make agreements with the enemy. The questions move progressively into more personal issues in your own life. This could be the beginning of breaking off things in your life that keep you down. I pray this is so.

1. Review pages 118-119 in the book that concern making agreements with the enemy. I want you to see this! Consider what types of agreements you or someone in general might make with the enemy. What does it look like? Jot your thoughts here.

2. Of the ways we make contracts with the enemy, which areas are you susceptible to?

3. Go through each of the seven things listed on pages118-119. Think about some of your own silent strongholds, forged as a result of painful childhood memories or overheard words. Write down here whatever comes to mind

Chapter 17. A Rescue Operation

1. After reading the explanation of Mark 3:27 on page 121 in the book, write in your own words what the verse is saying to you.

2. As you are reading this chapter, are any agreements or vows you may have made in your lifetime coming to mind? If so, write down what you are hearing.

3. Traumas in life come in all shapes and forms. It may come in the form of words from someone you trusted like, *"We never wanted you. You are so difficult to be with. You always…; You never…"* It could show up in some form of abuse whether mental, emotional or physical. Also, consider other kinds of trauma: being involved in an accident, seeing an accident happen, or witnessing of some traumatic event such as a terrorist act or a mass shooting. Remember, we all have many traumas over the course of a lifetime. As you think back over your life, what comes to your mind?

4. What emotions do you think or feel are attached to the traumas you wrote about above?

5. Review and summarize the steps I went through in my journey to break off praying through fear. Read Luke 9:1-2. What authority do you have as a believer in these areas of your life?

6. Does anything in your soul come to mind that may need to be broken off? Write it here and consider praying through this area to break off any agreements with the enemy.

What you have noted in the questions above are what the Spirit may be revealing. This is where you begin to pray and take authority as outlined in Chapter 5. Keep in mind, however, that you may need more help than this book provides. If you believe that is the case, stop now and put together a plan on where to go for help or who to call. Start with a trusted friend, a Pastor, a Bible Study leader or a mentor in your life. Then, once you have a plan, **DO. THE. WORK.** Take the steps you have outlined and pray over them. Offer them up to God asking for His help on leading you through this. Finally, do not *"wait until a more convenient time"*. Begin now. You know by now the enemy will try to steal the plan.

Part 2: Stepping In

This is a good place to stop and review Part 1. What have you learned? What principles do you need to cement into your soul? Make a list here.

Chapter 18. The Power Struggle

1. *"God uses everything in our past to bring us to the present and compel us into our future".* (Page 131) What things in your past can God use to minister to others in your present or future? Remember, we all have a story.

2. In the book you were asked on page 132 to make a list of every weapon mentioned in Ephesians 6:10-21. In this place, let's make a short commentary you can return to in the future. Write down:

   (a) Each weapon noted in the book.

   (b) What I learned about each weapon that will help me.

39

(c) Other insights I've gained in this area.

This will help you in the chapters that follow as well as in life in general. After writing and researching this section, I have gone back numerous times since. I have reviewed not just the weapon, but *how to use it!* It is part of our war training.

3. What are the two principles talked about in Ephesians 6:10-11. (Page 133) Why are they important?

4. Why do we need to put on the armor every day?

Review Ephesians 6:12-13 and the section describing it in the book.(Pages 135-138) It may be one of the most important parts of the book. Describe what happens to the loser in a wrestling match or struggle (in Ancient Greece). This explains for me why we are often unable to see clearly. Consider this concept prayerfully in your own life. Perhaps spiritual blindness has covered you because of things happening (or have happened) in your life. Thankfully, we know of One who can restore sight.

5. As you consider the list on page 136 describing the enemy, perhaps your eyes are already opening. Which of the Scripture verses exposes the enemy in a way you may not have seen before?

Chapter 19. Armor Up, We're Going In!

1. List the weapons mentioned in this chapter. Describe each weapon's purpose and how you see it operating in your life.

2. For each weapon mentioned in this chapter, what spiritual application can you make from the physical descriptions given? That is, what spiritual significance do you see from the belt's loops, empty compartments and capacity to hold equipment?

3. Regarding the shield of faith described on pages 141-142, what fiery darts are you most susceptible to? In other words, what areas in your life area you most vulnerable to attacks on your faith?

4. Review your answer to question three above. What strategies do you think would help you the next time these issues come up?

5. Go through chapters 18 and 19, writing down the three word summaries listed at the end of each section (i.e. **KNOW. THE. WORD.**) (Pages 135, 140 [occurs twice], 141, 142, 144, 147) Let these three word summaries remind you of how we get truth from our head to our heart.

Chapter 20. The Killing Sword

1. Who do you trust to walk through the battles of life with you? (Who is in your platoon?)

2. Read Linda's quote on page 148. What do you see as the best way you can *"develop better listening skills"*?

3. In the book I describe several ways to get Scripture from your head to your heart. Of the four ways mentioned on 148, which helps you the most? Can you think of other ways not mentioned?

4. What do you learn about *"Reading Devotionally"* (Pages 150-152) and *"Reading to Study"* (Pages 152-153)? What one thing can you incorporate into your own time with God?

5. What staff (page 153-154) do you need to pick up right now for your current place in the journey? Remember, faith turns promises into prophecy in your life.

Chapter 21. The Believer's Umbrella

1. I love Linda's walkie-talkie story on pages 155-156. What principles about prayer can you learn from this example?

2. Summarize the bullet points concerning *all kinds of prayer* on pages 157-158. Which types of prayer do you need to add to your arsenal?

3. Look at your summary in question 2. What different types of prayers have been answered in your life? Can you give an example?

4. How is Paul's prayer in Ephesians 6:19-20 an example to adopt for your own journey? (Pages 159-160)

5. Review the suggestions for developing your prayer life on pages 160-162. Which ones speak to your soul? What suggestions would you add to the list?

Read aloud the prayer by Oswald Chambers at the close of the chapter. Make it yours.

Chapter 22. Receiving and Setting Free

1. On page 167 I use the visual of a jailer (you) and a prisoner (one who has wronged you) as a picture of unforgiveness. There are many creative images we could use to describe this concept. Can you think of another visual that can explain what it looks like from your perspective?

2. Describe *vertical* forgiveness (Pages 168-170), in your own words?

3. Going through the book, make a list of points that describe how to receive *vertical* forgiveness.

4. Describe *horizontal* forgiveness on page 170, in your own words.

5. Going through the book, make a list of points that describe how to receive *horizontal* forgiveness.

6. As you read the story of the ear fungus and how the *fungus of unforgiveness* may cause a root of bitterness, take stock of your own situation. Are you experiencing bitterness from perhaps a long-term relationship? Or perhaps the pain of some sin against you. Are you harboring unforgiveness against God or someone else? Be aware and listen for a nudge concerning unexpected areas that might arise needing forgiveness. Jot down thoughts that come to you as you ponder the questions related here.

7. As you go through the bullet points listed on pages 172-174, which ones resonate with you?

Chapter 23. Mending Tears in the Fabric of the Soul

1. Why do you think it is necessary to repent and confess sin (1 John 1:9) if all of our sin was taken care of at the moment of salvation?

2. Write your definition of repentance here. Does it include all the elements of our words/attitudes/actions? (Page 179)

3. What do you learn about repentance by reading Judas' story on pages 179-181?

4. How would you describe the difference between repentance and confession?

5. Do you think both repentance and confession are necessary?

Chapter 24. Cleansing a Repentant Heart

1. Review the questions and your answers to Psalm 51 on page 184. What one thing did you learn from reading the psalm that you may not have known before.

2. Review the questions and your answers to Psalm 32 on pages 184-184. What one thing did you learn from reading the psalm that you may not have known before.

3. Review the questions and your answers to Psalm 38 on page 185. What one thing did you learn from reading the psalm that you may not have known before.

4. Describe the physical connection between sin and health.(Pages 185-186)

5. Under the section, *The Cleansing Agent* on page 186, write down your understanding of the power of the blood of Christ.

6. What is the "blood covenant" described on page 187?

7. How is Christ's blood the mending agent? (Pages 188-189)

8. Read through the definition of *perfect* on pages 188-189. Write down the meaning of the word. Summarize in your own words what it means to be *made perfect* by the blood of Christ.

Chapter 25. Oxygen for the Soul

1. How is worship a weapon of war? Why do you think it is one, if you do?

2. What *words, actions* and *attitudes* do you find yourself expressing in worship toward God? (Pages 191-193)

3. Craft your own definition of worship after reviewing the definitions provided on pages 193-194.

4. What additional concepts from your own experience can you provide to help you understand worship.

5. What elements of worship that you read about in this chapter can you incorporate into your own times of worship?

Chapter 26. The Heart of Worship

1. Review the story of the woman at the well in John 4:4-42. Record your insights about worship after your reading.

2. The book notes that the Jews avoided the route to Samaria because of a long-standing hatred toward Samaritans. Yet Jesus purposefully chose the route. (Page 198) Is there a place or a people you fail to consider because of some bias?

3. How do you experience the Living Water Christ provides? (Pages 198-199)

4. What was standing in the way of the woman's ability to receive the living water Christ offered? (John 4:16-20) (Pages 201-204) Is anything standing in your way?

5. We all have areas in life that we have not yet allowed Christ to fill. Turn the searchlight inward and ask the Holy Spirit to reveal what things you turn to in life to fill your emptiness. What do you see?

6. The woman's life shifted after Jesus exposed her sin. It was in her cry for help about where to worship. Jesus saw the real questions in her soul: *"How do I get more of Jesus' living water in my soul?"* What would *more* look like in your soul?

7. What does it mean to "worship in spirit and in truth"? (page 205)

8. Why do you think Jesus revealed who He was to this lowly, abused, lonely street woman?

9. What was the progression of change in the woman noted by the people of the town? (Page 207-208). Add your own insights. How does her journey translate to yours?

10. What did her change have to do with worship?

11. What is Jesus' thirst? (Pages 207)

Chapter 27. Secret Weapons in God's Army

1. Using the example of praying a Psalm on page 211, choose a Psalm you like and try the exercise. Write down what Psalm you chose and any insights in doing the assignment here.

2. We all have days when we don't *feel like* praising God. But, as I have learned, *"These are the important days…"* Do you agree with this statement? If so, why do you think it is an important statement for the journey? (Pages 211-212)

3. Why is worship and praise such an important weapon in the believer's arsenal?

4. Do you or have you ever fasted? For what purpose did you fast and what was the outcome?

5. Fasting is considered a powerful weapon of war. Why would you think this is so?

Chapter 28. The Power of Remembering

1. Why do you think *remembering* is added to the list of weapons of war?

2. What specifically does God ask you to remember? How does it strengthen you?

3. What is one of your greatest moments of God showing up in your life?

4. We do not often think of keeping the Sabbath as a weapon of war, thinking of it as an Old Testament practice. Do you see it as a weapon of war? Why or why not? (Pages 218-221)

5. What ideas come to mind as you think about celebrating Sabbath in your life?

Chapter 29. Dirt Disasters

1. What elements of the dirt disaster parable do you see as having to do with your personal journey?

2. Take each element of the parable, and define and write down its applicability to you and your life journey:
   - The owner of the dirt company

   - The soil

   - The seedlings

   - The water

   - The nutrients

   - The enemies

3. Do you see other elements not discussed in the chapter? Write about them here.

4. What does Luke instruct us about the heart in Luke 24:35-36.

Chapter 30. An Orphan's Journey to True Identity

1. Jot down any insights you gained from reading about Gideon's life.

2. Review and write down the weapons of war God gave to Gideon's army (beginning on page 229). What principles do you see here that can carry into your own life?

3. How is humility defined? (Page 232). Review 1 Peter 5:6 to further assist you.

4. What other Biblical examples of humility come to mind?

5. What do you think it means to *surrender fully* to God? (Pages 234-236)

6. Of the brief stories given about past followers of Jesus, which did you connect with the most? (Page 236)

7. Read Deuteronomy 30:19-20. What does God ask of you? What is your choice?

8. As a wrap to this study, what is the key to understanding why you are not experiencing the abundant life?

9. What changes have you already incorporated into your life and what changes do you see in your future to experience more fully the life Jesus promised?

Notes for Facilitators

Help for Group Facilitators

There is a difference between teaching and facilitating a study. This study guide is meant to be facilitated – giving everyone the opportunity to speak and share their own journey. If you are the chosen facilitator or the task just happens to fall to you, receive the assignment with anticipation that God will give you insights needed to fulfill His purposes for *each person* in the group, including yourself.

You do not need to be a Bible expert or a gifted teacher to lead a small group discussion. Your job is to help people discover for themselves what the Bible has to say and lead the group to listen attentively to themselves and each other as they make discoveries in their lives.

Plan to spend the minimum of an hour, depending on the size of the group, to go through the questions. You may need to pace the lessons after trying different methods. Some groups may want to do two or more lessons per session. Make this a group decision. It is always a good idea to leave room for prayer and praise time.

The first question of this guide asks each individual to come up with *one prayer request* that they want the group to pray for during the duration of the time together. Encourage each member to come up with a prayer request concerning their journey and what they hope or expect to receive from God.

Once a time is set, always begin and end on time. Look at the suggestions below to help you get more clarification.

69

Study Guide: Stepping Out – A Journey of the Soul

1. Before the group meeting, go through the study questions and the book, making a note of which exact page and section of the book is being noted in the question. This will help everyone find the place in the book where suggestions and answers might be found.

2. NEVER ask anyone to pray aloud or read aloud unless you are ABSOLUTELY CERTAIN they are comfortable doing it.

3. One of the most important concepts the group needs to agree on at the beginning is that *what is shared in the group stays in the group*. More than one person in the Body of Christ has been deeply wounded and critically injured by indiscriminate "sharing" outside the group of personal information without permission. This is so very critical to understand and agree on. Please, please, please be very careful here. We are holding each others' hearts. Be like Jesus in this area!

4. Make sure you as the facilitator do not do all the talking. Balance it out to make sure that you too have time to share your own thoughts, but do not lead the question with your answer. Don't be afraid of silence. People may need time to think about the question before speaking.

5. Ask God to help you understand the question or passage being discussed. I suggest you read over each Scripture verse mentioned before the group time.

6. At the beginning of the first session together, explain that this meeting is meant to be a discussion not a lecture and

that each person, according to their comfort level, should feel free to share.

7. You may want to discuss at the beginning concerns about making sure everyone has a chance to speak. As a group leader, you may run into issues where one or two people take up most of the time with their own issues. Other people who do not have a chance to speak may not feel comfortable sharing, or may just quietly leave the group. The best way to handle this is to seat yourself next to a talker, not across from them. Studies have shown that known talkers often contribute less if they do not have eye contact with the leader. If that fails, you may need to pull the person aside and gently ask them to hold back and let other less verbal people share first.

8. In your discretion, take turns reading the questions and the Scripture verses aloud. Some Bible verses might be too long. In that case, assure that everyone has read the verses before beginning the discussion.

9. Sometimes groups get off track of the questions they are discussing. In the law, we call these "red herrings". When that happens, discern whether the direction is of positive value to the whole group. If related to the topic at hand, you might allow the deviation. To get back on track, simply ask, at an appropriate break, if anyone else has a response to question X.

10. There are times when an upcoming question might already have been answered through the prior discussion. In that case, move on to the next question or ask if

anyone else has a response they wish to bring up before moving on.

11. This study guide does not cover every element in the book. Thus, there are times when a member might have a question not addressed in the study guide. Feel free to see how you or others respond to their question before moving on.

12. Never be content with one answer. Always ask others if they have input into the question. In this type of study, every heart needs an opportunity to be heard. On the other hand, do not demand that anyone answer a particular question. Some of the questions are personal to the heart of each person. Some may not be comfortable at this time sharing. You might consider a class at the end as a *catch-up* to go back and see if anyone wants to share something they passed by the first time around.

13. The purpose of this study is NOT to get through the questions. It is to hear each other's heart and the painful and positive things each person is experiencing. Helping people speak of these things helps each of us align them in our souls and move from head to heart.

14. If you feel able, you might on occasion want to summarize what the members have said about a particular passage or question. It will help build unity and give continuity to the study. Be careful of sounding like you're taking over.

15. Most importantly, acknowledge each person's contribution with a positive response: *"Good summary; good point; thank you for sharing that; very insightful."*

16. If the contribution is clearly not relevant or blatantly untrue, instead of confronting, ask the person, *"That is an interesting observation. What thoughts or verses led you to this conclusion?"* Or ask the group, *"What do the rest of you think?"* But be very careful not to gang up or attack the person. This is heart stuff we are dealing with. We are all fragile.

17. Remember that not everyone will agree on every point. Some points in the book may be controversial to the members of the group. Rather than rag on the author (me, in that case) or a member of the group who may agree or disagree with the rest of the group, talk through the points in a logical but loving manner. In the end, agree to disagree if the subject gets too hot and group members are feeling agitated or uncomfortable. We are all members of one body and need each other. It is okay to agree to disagree. Recommend that each member pray and be open to what *God says* – not me, you or someone else in the group.

18. Always conclude with prayer. End on time. Expect and pray for God's blessing. Do not forget to Praise Him for His goodness.

Study Guide: Stepping Out – A Journey of the Soul

For more information about Kim's writing and speaking ministry, www.kingsagenda.com or contact Kim at:

kimpublish@earthlink.net

Include your testimony or share about help or encouragement you received from this study. Your prayer requests are also welcome. I *will* pray for you.

www.ingramcontent.com/pod-product-compliance
Lightning Source LLC
Chambersburg PA
CBHW071837020426
42331CB00007B/1765